# Disney PRINCESS

# Tangled

# It's Better When You Sing It

## A Musical Exploration Storybook

HAL•LEONARD®

Explore an interactive experience online! Go to:
www.halleonard.com/exploremusic/00160408

Printed in the United States of America

ISBN 978-1-4950-6477-7

Published by Hal Leonard LLC
7777 W. Bluemound Road
P.O. Box 13819
Milwaukee, WI 53213

# CONTENTS

Rapunzel loved to sing. When she was in her tower painting, knitting, or making music, she sang songs to her little friend Pascal, the chameleon. It was always more fun when she sang.

**IT'S BETTER WHEN YOU SING IT!**

What can you do while you are singing?

Rapunzel kept herself very busy.
Sometimes she sat quietly. Other
times she rushed around very fast.

The speed of a song
is called *tempo*.

You can sing a song in
a slow or fast tempo.

Try it with
"Twinkle, Twinkle, Little Star."
First, sing it slow:

*Twinkle, twinkle, little star,*
*How I wonder what you are.*

Now try it fast!

Rapunzel's tower
reached from
low to high.

You have a high voice
and a low voice.

*This is my high voice.*
*This is my low voice.*

Make your voice
slide from high to low.

*Wooooo!*

Now slide from
low to high!

*Wooooo!*

Make your voice slide from
low to high to low again.

*Wooooo!*

Rapunzel had always dreamed of leaving the
tower, but when the moment came, she was
frightened. She hesitated for a moment, then
her foot touched the soft grass. To her surprise,
she was actually in the outside world.

Your voice is your very own instrument. You can sound your best when you take lots of air into your lungs and open your mouth wide.

Imagine stepping on the ground for the first time after being locked in a tower. Take a surprised breath, open your mouth wide, and sing:

*Ahhhhhh!*

When Rapunzel was in the tower with Mother Gothel, she used her voice to speak or whisper. When she skipped through the forest or swung across a river on a vine, she used her voice to sing and shout.

Use your voice to speak, whisper, shout, and sing.

*This is my speaking voice.*
*This is my whispering voice.*
*This is my shouting voice.*
*This is my singing voice.*

Rapunzel was excited to see and hear the world around her. She heard birds chirping, frogs croaking, the sound of a gurgling brook, and the wind in the trees.

You can take a "sound walk." When you walk to the park or playground, listen to the sounds all around you.

Can you imitate those sounds with your own voice?

Try it in your house for an inside "sound walk."

Rapunzel made friends with the small furry creatures in the forest and played a game with them.

**IT'S BETTER WHEN YOU SING IT!**

You can play a singing game with friends or family members.

*Yoo-hoo, where are you?*

*Here I am.*

Follow the sound of their voice to find them!

In the pub, Rapunzel helped the men
sing about their dreams. She sang about
her own dreams too.

Create your own song
by adding new words to
a tune you already know.

*Everybody has a dream,*
*Share your dream*
*with me.*

When Rapunzel saw the kingdom for the first time, she heard the church bells ringing and all the sounds of the village. There were so many different sounds to hear. Music was in the air and all around!

Songs can help you express your feelings.

How would you sing this?

*Today is my birthday!*

How would you sing this?

*It's raining.
I can't go outside today.*

What other feelings can you express by singing?

Rapunzel walked through the gates of the kingdom and entered the village. There was a festival with music and dancing. The children rushed up to her, and Rapunzel greeted them all.

You can learn a song
by echoing what you hear:

1, 2, 3, *sing with me.*
    1, 2, 3, *sing with me.*

1, 2, 3, *dance with me.*
    1, 2, 3, *dance with me.*

*Reach up high.*
    *Reach up high.*

*Reach down low.*
    *Reach down low.*

*Say goodbye.*
    *Say goodbye.*

*Off we go.*
    *Off we go.*

Flynn led Rapunzel to a boat and rowed them to a spot with a perfect view of the kingdom. As the lanterns floated into the sky, they sang a song to each other. It was the perfect ending to a perfect day.

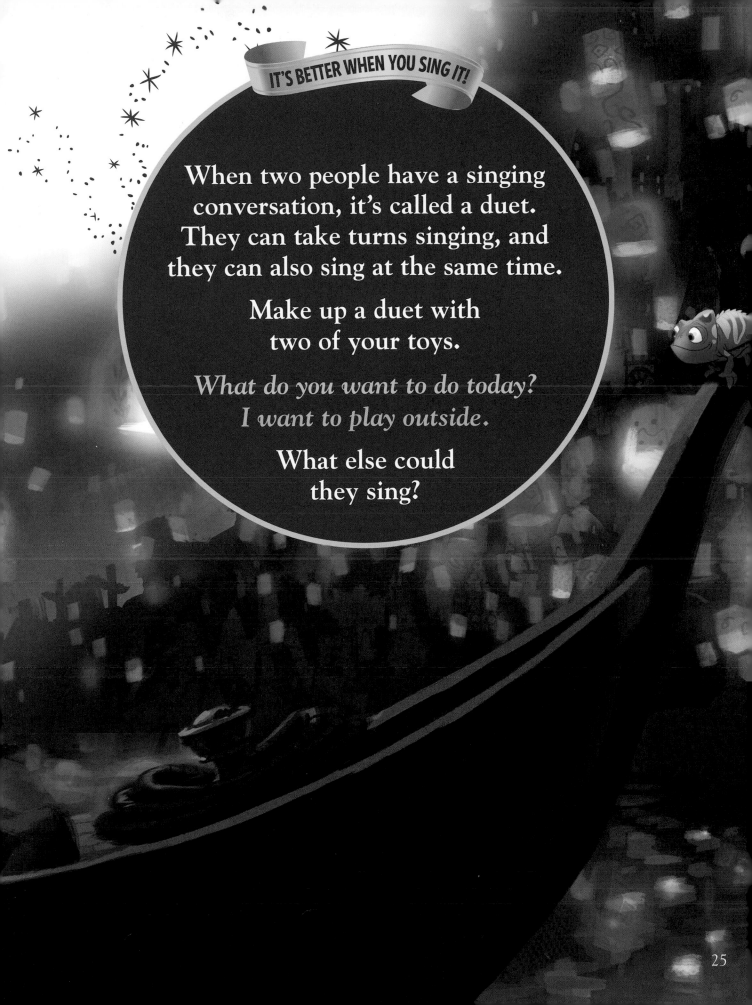

When two people have a singing conversation, it's called a duet. They can take turns singing, and they can also sing at the same time.

Make up a duet with two of your toys.

*What do you want to do today?*
*I want to play outside.*

What else could they sing?

# WHAT DID YOU LEARN?

**Singing is fun.**
Page 4

**You can sing fast and slow.**
Page 6

**You can sing high and low.**
Page 8

**Take a breath, open wide, and sing!**
Page 10

**You have four voices: speaking, whispering, shouting, and singing.**
Page 12

You can listen
to the sounds
around you.
Page 14

You can sing
a hide-and-seek
game.
Page 16

You can
make up your
own song.
Page 18

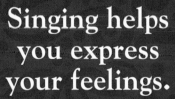

Singing helps
you express
your feelings.
Page 20

You can
echo a song.
Page22

Two singers
can sing a duet.
Page 24

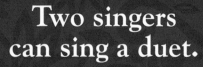

**Go online for more activities**
www.halleonard.com/exploremusic/00160408

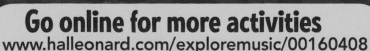

# IT'S BETTER WHEN YOU SING IT

Listen to the music.

Music is in the air.

Can you hear the music?

You know, it might be anywhere.

No need to look far and wide,

You'll find your own voice deep inside,

Just let it out.

Don't let it hide,

And you'll be glad you tried!

It's better when you sing it. Wo-oh,

Better when you sing it. Wo-oh,

Better when you sing it. Wo-oh,

So let's all sing our song.

It's better when you sing it. Wo-oh,

Better when you sing it. Wo-oh,

Better when you sing it. Wo-oh,

Come on now, everybody sing along.

Everybody sing along.

**Sing along online**
www.halleonard.com/exploremusic/00160408

Let's sing high!

(Echo) Let's sing high!

And we can sing low!

(Echo) And we can sing low!

Let's sing very, very, very, very fast!

(Echo) Let's sing very, very, very, very fast!

Then slow.

(Echo) Then slow.

Just know, wherever you go:


It's better when you sing it. Wo-oh,

Better when you sing it. Wo-oh,

Better when you sing it. Wo-oh,

So let's all sing our song.

It's better when you sing it. Wo-oh,

Better when you sing it. Wo-oh,

Better when you sing it. Wo-oh,

Come on now, everybody sing along.

Come on now, everybody sing along.

Everybody sing along!

# GLOSSARY

**duet** – two people singing

**echo** – same sound repeated back

**fast** – moving with more speed

**high** – music sounds that are above others

**low** – music sounds that are below others

**shouting voice** – loud voice used to show excitement or to get someone's attention

**singing voice** – voice for making music

**slow** – moving with less speed

**speaking voice** – talking voice

**tempo** – speed of the music

**whispering voice** – quiet speaking voice

# TO PARENTS AND CAREGIVERS

Singing and music play an important role in the life of a child. Not only does music help children to express themselves, but it also provides significant benefits to a child's growth and development.

Because the ability to sing is innate, children often naturally begin to sing in their toddler years, as auditory and speech skills quickly develop. Sing to your child anytime and as often as possible. As you do, toddlers and preschoolers will mimic you and will want to sing simply because it's fun to do.

Young children are not self-conscious about singing. They love to do it! They especially enjoy singing songs that:

• repeat words and melodies

• include words that encourage movement

• contain a strong steady beat

• talk about animals, toys, or familiar people (family, friends)

How can I help my child enjoy music and singing?

• Sing to your child often. Make it part of your natural routine.

• Play echo games. Sing a phrase of a song and wait for your child to echo.

• Watch movies and TV programs with your child and learn some songs together.

• Sing instructions to your child using familiar tunes
 (for example, "Mary Had a Little Lamb").

• Help your child recognize others who sing (on the radio, on TV, in the movies, at concerts, at church, etc.).

• Compliment and encourage your child whenever you hear him/her sing.

Sing and make music with your child every day! It's a wonderful way to bond and nurture physical, emotional, and social development.

Access online content:
**www.halleonard.com/exploremusic/00160408**